Lifelong L-Earning

Breaking Down Your Personal Financial Game Plan

Dr Julie Bonner

ISBN: 0989203948
ISBN-13: 978-0989203944

DEDICATION

This work is dedicated to the process of personal financial planning for all of those who feel financial planning is boring or something that is too intimidating to accomplish. For anyone to be good at any endeavor you need the ability to learn. As long as you have the ability to learn, you can increase your earning potential and achieve any financial goal!

Table of Contents

ACKNOWLEDGMENTS

Thank you to my parents who, through very tough love, forced me to learn about personal financial management. It started my own learning journey, and the more I learned, the more I feel empowered in my life.

PREFACE

On July 24, 1938, S. J. Woolf wrote an article that appeared in the New York Times based on an interview with Henry Ford called "Henry Ford, at 75, States his Faith Simply". One nugget of wisdom he shared was about experience – that our experience was "the one thing no one can take away from us". As you read, experience, and apply the information in this book, remember this, once you know something and can apply that knowledge, no one can ever take that away from you. Learning how to L-EARN is the single biggest gift of empowerment you can ever give yourself.

Why is this so important? Allow me to describe an encounter I experienced as a financial planner. I had received a lead from our database – a woman in her 50's, and when we met, she admitted that she had never really thought about retirement, but now she wanted to retire in less than ten years. Therefore, she had virtually nothing saved in her 401-k and all she would really have to live on would be social security benefits.

A few things were disheartening about this scenario. First, she had never empowered herself to learn, and I will never know why she never learned. Perhaps she felt that financial matters were too technical or hard to understand. Perhaps she had people around her telling her she would never have to understand these things because her husband would take care of it. Regardless, she came into the office with no idea what to do.

Second, the company that I worked for, of course, works off of commissions, so she was not seen as a lucrative client and I was discouraged to take her on. My desire at the time was to teach her, but that is not really the role of the financial planner. They have information to share and they are willing to educate, but clients have to come in with some knowledge of their own plan and how to achieve that plan and understand the financial incentives of the planners.

Do not allow this scenario to happen to you. Money is so crucial to your standard of living, to your peace of mind, to your feeling of security that you owe it to yourself to learn how to l-earn. This book is not a book about all of the different kinds of investments you can do nor is it a complete comparison of all kinds of financial instruments. No, instead it is a book that teaches you how to think about your financial plan and how to put one together for yourself. Never, ever give your power to someone else on managing your plan – a financial planner works for you, on your team, but the financial planner or any other member of your team should never discount your wishes or input. This is about YOUR money, YOUR life,

YOUR decisions – not theirs.

The book is written in small "pieces" so that over time, as you work through each section, you will have compiled all of the information necessary for your own personal financial plan. A plan, in my terms, is not a static document. It is a dynamic, living document that is to be changed as you learn and grow in your financial prowess.

Finally, the learning process works like this:

Analyze what is so about your current state

Set **goals** for where you want to be

Determine **how** you will achieve the goals and collect feedback

Implement the plan

Collect **feedback** and continuously l-earn

As you learn about the process of financial planning, you will actively address each of these l-earning steps, and by the time you are done, you will have a personal financial plan that you can manage for the rest of your life.

This book will not tell you what to invest in, but it will help you to learn about what personal financial planning is all about, and depending on your learning style, you can craft a financial plan that works for you for the long term. The book is written to highlight items that should be considered, but depending on your temperament, style, risk profile, and interest, certain things you may decide not to do. In the end, you have to own the decisions you make about this important aspect of your life – this is a framework on how to think about it to enable yourself to make those decisions.

INTRODUCTION

If your family is like mine, I never really knew about the financial worries or successes of my parents. Every now and again, I would hear certain things, and they wanted me to be conscientious with money, but I really did not get an in depth insight into how they thought and felt about money.

I do know a few things – they had gotten into an overdraft situation early in their marriage because they did not discuss or keep track of their money, and they vowed that would never happen again. I always saw my mom reconciling her checkbook.

I, like many of you, had to learn a lot on my own. Truth is, your situation could be very different than your parents, which will cause you to have to learn about investment instruments perhaps they knew nothing about. But, there are many things you can learn if you are comfortable with the process of learning.

In fact, I have taught financial planning for several years, and one thing rings true with every group. Over half of the group will have never known about the bulk of the topics contained in a financial plan. Even fewer have put together a plan. Once they see that it is not difficult, once they see it is a learning process, they can relax and get into the flow. In fact, if people are like me, there is NOTHING I hate worse than feeling like I am incompetent. However, when it comes to financial planning I notice that feeling and continue learning in spite of that feeling, otherwise you can get stuck never exploring financial possibilities.

In fact, I will even be more honest. I have always been interested in financial topics and I saw as a financial advisor the power of investing in options. I learned the basics of options in 2003. However, it was not until 2010 that I felt comfortable investing my own money in options. Over that seven year time frame, I had big gaps of time where I did not read or study about this topic, but then there would be long stretches where I would look for everything I could read on the subject. Eventually I practiced with virtual money and that is when my learning took off and then I started making money with options.

In my first foray in options, a person could earn maybe 1% a year on a savings account, but I was earning an average of 20% per year investing in options. My learning approach paid off.

The other concern I hear from students is that this takes too much time. Learning how to do can take time, but you can work on sections and pieces in shorter periods of time. Plus, not everything will interest you when it comes to a financial plan. Perhaps, some things will not even apply to you.

You can figure out your own schedule, based on your needs. It used to be that I only touched up and refined my plan once a year. I had gotten into the habit of taking January 1 as my celebrating successes day, goal setting day, and assessing where I was in my financial plan. It is not that I was not aware of things the rest of the year; it is just that I formally updated the document on January 1. I have also experimented with looking at these documents once a quarter. In the end, your cadence is up to you.

The way this book is structured is that each chapter and each topic is the outline of your financial plan. There will be learning prompts at the end of each chapter where you can take those and assess your situation, identify gaps in your knowledge, and make action plans.

Take as long as you need with a section. You could spend an hour on gathering your financial documents, a month, or a year to get it completed. Try not to be a perfectionist – that is another feeling that can get in your way of progress. Take it at your own pace!

FINANCIAL DOCUMENTS

The place to start with any financial plan is to gather your financial information and documentation. Your financial plan starts with knowing all of your income sources, investments, bank information, expenses, websites, etc. Let us tackle one category at a time.

Income Sources

First, what are your income sources? For some, there is one or two income sources, but you could have several places where you earn income. Essential information to collect about your income sources:

1. Name of the company or source
2. The timing of the pay details (i.e., weekly, monthly, or some other trigger that generates a check or deposit to your bank account)
3. Telephone numbers and addresses of the income source
4. Year-end tax document (W-2, 1099, or other type)
5. Website, if applicable
6. Log in credentials to the website

Expenses

Second, identify and list out all of the expenses that are incurred. The important characteristics of this list are recurring expenses that occur every month, or every other month, quarterly, or yearly. This list will likely be more extensive, but you will want to capture the following information:

1. Company name
2. Address and telephone numbers
3. Account numbers
4. Website information
5. Login credentials
6. How is the expense paid (i.e., credit card, auto withdrawal, check)
7. Timing of expense (i.e., paid every other month, monthly, yearly, etc.)

Credit and Debit Cards

Third, identify all of your credit cards and debit cards. Capture the following information regarding these cards:

1. Bank name
2. Telephone number and address
3. Benefits gained (i.e., cash back, points, etc.)
4. Annual interest rate
5. Due date
6. Website
7. Login credentials

Investments

Fourth, list out all of your investment accounts. This can include many different flavors of investments like savings accounts, brokerage accounts, employer sponsored plans like 401-k's, Roth IRA's, and other types of retirement plans. Capture information regarding these accounts to include:

1. Company name and contact information
2. Website
3. Type of account
4. Login credentials

Insurance

Fifth, list out all of your insurance products that you carry. Insurance can be life, disability, car, home or apartment, pet, long term care, etc. Include the following information:

1. Company name and contact information
2. Find a copy of the policy or call the company to get one
3. Premium amount

4. Timing of payment

Finally, have a copy of your will, powers of attorney, living revocable trust, and an advanced directive. All of these important documents I have asked you to gather need to be somewhere where you can get your hands on them and where they are protected. For example, you can get a lockbox at the bank or you can obtain a fireproof safe for your home. Either way, have the documents under lock and key for safe keeping (or password protected if you use Excel or an application for your smart phone or tablet).

L-Earning Prompts – Financial Documents

Do you have all of these documents and websites identified?

How will you collect this information?

Where will you store the information?

Who will you inform of where this information is located?

How much security over this information do you desire?

MATTERS OF HEART AND MIND

Your past and present inform your future. Sometimes, people can be unaware of the subtle power belief systems and emotions can have on your financial decision making. I mention this now because as you compile your financial information and documents, you could have all manner of feelings and thoughts start to erode your confidence.

If, over time, you find yourself procrastinating on taking action, or if you are just not achieving the goals you want to achieve, take a hard look at your money history. Sometimes, we believe that we should not want money, or that we should not talk about money, or that we are told we would never be good with money.

Since money affects all aspects of your life, it is wise to know what money messages you received, or what you decided about money based on experiences you saw other go through. For example, we often follow in our parents footsteps and model after or rebel against their behavior. Did your parents save? Did they exhibit behaviors of being tight with money or overly free with money? Did any of their behaviors give your parents good things but cause you to go without food or other necessities?

Whatever you have experienced, even as an adult, can cause you to make certain decisions about money that may not be useful to you. An example of this can be when the market turns sour and you lose some money in stocks that you own. What you decide this means is important for the future, because it can cause you to decide that stocks are not for you. This decision/conclusion may or may not be true.

The key to any experience you have is to learn from it and decide consciously what you will adjust in your plan. Emotions are good feedback mechanisms and use them as such – and never give over your authority to unconsciousness.

Finally, habits can be good or bad. We have habits so that they can make us more efficient. The important thing is to have habits that help you achieve your goals. If you are not achieving the goal, then you could have a bad habit ingrained in your behavior. There is an excellent book called *The Richest Man in Babylon*, by George Samuel Clason, originally published in 1926 that is an interesting read that has a story in it about how debt makes you a slave. To get out of that slavery requires a mindset shift.

In fact, many will talk about good debt versus bad debt. This is a great conversation to have, and for the most part I agree with it. However, if you are starting to stress out about money, even good debt can have negative consequences for your life, your health, and your psyche.

Your Mind Works for YOU

Maybe you have noticed this, but your mind is sometimes not your friend. Therefore, if you do not understand how the mind can trap you into bad habits or how the mind can get you enslaved to debt then you are at the whim of your brain and how it functions. We tend to think, and we want to think, that our brains are logical, and we appear to want to think sometimes that if we can eliminate emotion from our thinking and decision-making then we would be ok.

We actually do need emotions to make better decisions. A good resource on this subject is a book called *How We Decide*, by Jonah Lehrer. The important thing to note about how the mind works is that the brain is processing logic as well as emotion – there are parts of the brain that regulate both of these and we have to be smarter about how we manage the brain and its reactions to stimulus.

This is why it is important to note that when we have something traumatic happen, the brain will infuse that experience in our thinking and the conclusion we draw can get cemented in our behavior. This can be a good thing or a bad thing or a neutral thing, depending on the circumstances.

Personally, I have discovered over the years that I have to pay close attention to what my brain tells me. Allow me to give context for what I am about to express: Several years ago, I attended a money seminar (http://bit.ly/1hzSsf8) that was incredible with the insight I gained into the psychology of money. It was at that money seminar that I learned of a camp that would be conducted in the wilderness of the mountains of British Columbia, Canada. I wanted to go because I have always been a fan of personal growth and this seminar marketed the message that if there was anything blocking my success I would learn what it was in this seminar.

I have never served in the military, but I would imagine boot camp worked a lot like this – you got little sleep and were constantly challenged emotionally and physically during the five and a half day experience. I do not consider myself an athlete at all, but I was able to engage and keep up with the physical challenges. These included things like participating in physical challenges with a jujitsu master, scaling a mountain peak on a timed exercise, sitting in a sweat lodge for over three hours, and completing a forty foot long fire walk. By the time we had reached the final day of the camp, I was fairly pleased with how well I had been able to handle this physical exertion.

However, an interesting thing happened on the final day. We go to our physical challenge to find that we are facing a ropes course. Compared to the fire walk, the sweat lodge and other experiences, this appeared to be a cake walk! However, as we started, I experience literally two halves of my brain at war with each other.

One side of my brain was saying "Piece of cake, this is easy" and the other side of my brain was screaming "You're gonna die!" As we progressed through the activities, I found myself in front of one of them and I said to the facilitator, "My legs are killing me; I don't think I can climb anymore". He responded, "That is fine, I will hoist you up to the platform". He did that and as I was preparing to fly out through the tree canopy on the zip line, my brain said to me, "Look what a failure you are, you had to ask for help" – and this was NOT a kind voice, it was a mean and sarcastic voice dripping with disdain.

I was shocked….but went on with the zip line and then went to my final station. Again, I had to climb and was so unhappy to have to be climbing again that I was bound and determined not to do it because my legs and back were just howling in pain. My team would not allow me to sit out, so I slowly and painfully started climbing the ladder. I don't know how long it took, but it was a few minutes, because I am hurting, I am angry, and I am crying the whole way. As I get to the top of the ladder, my mind says to me, “Fine, you want to kill yourself then go ahead”.

In that moment, all the pain left me and I mean all of it. I no longer felt any pain in any region of my body. As I digested these messages afterward, I realized two things.

One, I had always heard my father say, “If you want something done right you have to do it yourself” – I had never realized just how much I had bought into this message. Was it possible that I was not a good team player? Was it possible that I would not allow others to help me? Was I missing out on the wisdom of others because I stubbornly held the belief that only I could do it best?

Second, I started to wonder if the brain was powerful enough that if I was getting outside of my comfort zone that the brain could manufacture a feeling of real pain. What I eventually found out was that it can! I was so surprised to learn that the brain has the power to trick you into believing a false reality. Not too long after this seminar, I was out following up on goals I had committed to during the camp and found that my back was in agony, and thus I was contemplating going home because of the physical pain. I then asked my brain is this real? Are you just making this up to get me to stop? I swear to you, my brain starting making excuses like a little kid caught with the hand in the cookie jar – and I knew right then and there that I really had to learn how to master my mind, or my mind would master me without my awareness.

Since then, I have used this technique of questioning to determine what I think is real pain, or real symptoms, and sometimes the brain reacts like that naughty little kid, and then sometimes, I have found that the symptoms I am feeling are accurate. That a cold might actually be coming on or that I truly do have a painful back.

The brain is the ruler of the flight or fight response. In those moments where you may want to spend money on something fun, or when you are trying to break what you think is a bad habit, the brain will sometimes try to sabotage you, so the more you know to challenge it, the more successful you will be.

Your Life as a Laboratory

When I teach, I often have students change up their habits. There are several reasons for this. One, sometimes the most mundane things can really give us fresh insight. Two, changing our habits can keep us in a more creative and resourceful frame of mind. Finally, habits can serve you but they can also hinder you.

When I have given this as an assignment, I will explain to students that they have to try at least one new tweak to one habit on each of four days of the week. They can repeat the one tweak, or they can change things up. For example, if you decided to drive to work a different way, you might actually forget to do it on the first day you want to try this tweak. Just notice that and try the same one again if you want to the next day. Or the next day you may try to drive to church a different way, or drive to class a different way, or do something else not even associated with driving.

One thing you may discover is that habits are so powerful; you may have to attempt this several times before you actually remember to do it. Now, driving to work the same way, every day, is not a bad thing. But until we play around with our habits, sometimes we may find something that actually serves us even better. Such as we may find a route that saves us even more time, or not, but this is how learning occurs.

Another thing I have suggested is for people to come up with their own tweaks that they want to do around habits. Students have come up with some interesting ones. For example, one person decided she wanted to be more positive in her speech. When she came to class, she told us about her experience and that her four year old son was really disturbed by her positive attitude. I asked her what she had learned and she said that she learned that she needed to remain negative in her speech. Now whether she decides to do that or not, I asked her if she would be willing to at least consider a different perspective on this conclusion. Basically, would she consider it, and she would not have to tell anyone of us if she actually considered it or not, and she agreed. Therefore, I asked her, which was more powerful – to remain in the habit and teach her son to be negative or to teach him how he can actually change a habit that maybe is not good for the long run?

The possibilities are endless on habits that can be tweaked. You can practice saying positive things about your money management skills – then notice how your mind may scoff at you each time you try, or you may notice that suddenly you feel more empowered. You can try to take $100 and put it in an envelope for your spending money for the week. You may be successful in spending only $100, or you may not, the key is to practice learning through the experience.

L-Earning Prompts – Heart and Mind

What are my money habits?

What money experiences impacted me positively or negatively?

What conclusions did I draw regarding those experiences?

Do my conclusions help me to achieve my goals or do they hinder me?

Do I not give myself enough credit to l-earn and grow?

Do I have more positive role models around me to leverage off of?

Have I trained my brain to be my partner?

What would I like to tweak this week, month, or year to learn more?

PERSONAL FINANCIAL STATEMENTS

Cash Flow

Cash flow is the income and outflow of your cash. This is why it is important to understand when your income is coming into your account and from what sources, but also to be aware of when the expenses are leaving your account.

There are many ways to handle this aspect of your financial statements and many advisors will tell you all you need is a budget. Personally, I have found that budgets are too rigid. In other words, I do budget, for example, I know that my electricity bill is around $100 a month and that is the amount I budget. So, in that sense, I do budget my money. But the key for me has been will I have enough money to cover that bill when it comes due? In order to make sure that I know the bill can be covered, I put all my income and expenses on a calendar spreadsheet. This way, I can project out for as many months as I desire and see the incoming money and the outflow of expenses to ensure that my expenses are covered.

The added benefit of this method is that I can also see what "free" money I have at any given point in time and how long that money is available to me to spend or save. Therefore, if I want to go to dinner, or go to a movie, or move that extra money into savings, I can make a solid decision on what should be done with the money.

Personally, Excel is a terrific tool to do this in – I find that I am most creative with setting up Excel to track most anything I want. This book is not a tutorial on how to use Excel, but I can work with you to set up your own tracking mechanisms. The reason I find it a better tool is that, yes, there are financial tracking tools out there, like Microsoft Money, Quicken, or Mint – but they are designed as the developers think you need them to be designed and there is little flexibility in those tools unless you can convince the developers that your idea is the next greatest thing for them to do a version change. Excel gives YOU the power, and I am all about empowerment. Nothing is perfect, but over time, I have found that I like to build my own trackers and that way, I never lose anything or miss something because I did not understand all of the functionality of the tool.

Timing of Income and Expenses

One thing to bear in mind as you study your inflow and outflow of money, you need to be aware of timing.

Most people are aware of having timing differences in payroll. For example, my father used to be paid on a weekly basis every Friday as an hourly worker. Some companies pay out salaries based on a schedule of the first and the fifteenth of the month. However, some companies pay out bi-weekly.

So what is the difference?

The big deal with this is that your expenses are often coming in every month. For example, even though I *could* pay my car insurance once every six months, I typically do not have that much extra money to pay my car insurance ahead like that, so I tend to pay it monthly. For the most part, your expenses will come in to be paid monthly.

Therefore, you want as much of your salary/payroll to be paid out each month as possible. Let's take a look at an example:

If your salary is $50,000 a year, and your company pays out on the first and the fifteenth of the month, then you would receive the following gross pay per month:

Over 12 months, you would be paid 24 times (12 months times 2 payouts). Thus, take your $50,000 salary and divide by 24 and you would be paid $2,083.33 each payday, or $4,166.67 per month ($2083.33 times 2).

Now compare that to a company that pays you every two weeks (or bi-weekly). This means, that each year has 52 weeks, and if you divide 52 by 2 you get 26 paychecks (versus 24 paychecks when you are paid on the first and the fifteenth of the month). That sounds good initially, but this actually causes you to have to live on less money throughout the year.

Why?

Because your $50,000 salary is now divided by 26, and that result is $1,923.08 per paycheck (gross). So ten months out of the year, you will receive two paychecks ($1,923.08 times 2 or $3,846.15) and two months out of the year, you will receive three paychecks (or $1,923.08 times 3 = $5,769.24).

So, let us compare…..if you are paid on the first and fifteenth, you will have a gross paycheck of $4,166.67 to live off of but if you are paid on a bi-weekly schedule you will have to live on $3,846.15 on ten months out of the year. And if you are lucky enough to have the discipline, you will bank that extra paycheck on the other two months for those gaps in your monthly spending – but how many of us have that discipline?

Often, this is a company decision, and there is not anything that can really be done about it unless a grass roots change happens with employees arguing for a different approach then you have to be aware of the difference and the impact that this can have on your planning.

Please see Excel Appendix for how Excel can be used to calculate cash flow.

Moving Due Dates

Another timing issue that can occur for you is to have the expenses not evenly distributed throughout the month. Sometimes, it may be impossible to even out your expenses, but separating them can often give you some breathing room.

You will know if you have this problem if you often lament, "in the first half of the month I feel flush with money, but then feel very strapped for cash as we get close to paying rent". This way, you can match up your expenses or align your expenses to the rhythm of the income that is coming into your bank account.

Physical Separation of Money

Some people struggle with budgeting and it may be because of the fact that it is just numbers on a page. I have seen strategies where some people have used multiple checking accounts to separate out money, or to have envelopes where they keep cash for certain purposes.

For example, I have tried both strategies and found them to be useful. The idea is this, if you have the money in your "dining out" envelope, then you can go out to dinner. If you do not have enough money in the envelope for dining out, then you can't go out to dinner. This was useful to me when I felt like I was starting to rely too much on credit cards – again, an awareness of a habit that perhaps was not helping me reach my financial goals.

Net Worth

Your net worth is an analysis of your assets and liabilities. These are the assets you have that can be turned into cash and the outstanding balances on loans and consumer credit that you owe. The important thing about this analysis is you want to determine if you have a positive net worth. Even if you have a negative net worth, because you just never knew how to do this, that is ok….you can fix it!

Your assets list would be things like the balances in your bank accounts (checking and savings), your investment balances, and the current market appraisal of your house.

Your liabilities list are the balances on your credit cards, outstanding balances owed on your car or mortgage or any other lines of credit, loans, etc.

You add up the total assets and subtract the total of your liabilities, and hopefully, you have more assets than liabilities. This is important because if you desire to leave assets to your family upon your death, if you have more liabilities than assets then your heirs will not see anything of your assets.

Personal Financial Ratios

Being aware of personal financial ratios are important because it helps you to know how a lending institution will view your financial position and financial acumen. Here are some to be aware of, now that you have set up your cash flow and your net worth:

Liquidity – Liquid Assets / Monthly Expenses

Liquid assets would be pulled from the assets list on your net worth statement. Generally, if you can turn an asset into cash within 90 days, it is a liquid asset.

Monthly expenses would come from your cash flow statement. The challenge sometimes is that not all bills come in on a monthly basis, so you can take historical data and do an average of your expenses per month.

In general, you want your liquidity ratio to be a solid 1 or better. This would mean that you have enough assets to take care of your expenses. You are starting to get into trouble if this ratio goes below a 1. You might be ok if this happens for a short while, but for the long term, having a number consistently below 1 is trouble.

Debt Ratio – Total Debt / Total Assets

Total Debt is taken from your net worth statement and this is the total of all the balances you owe on credit cards and loans.

Total Assets is also taken from your net worth statement (which will include the liquid assets).

This number you want to be smaller than 1. This is a common metric that creditors will look at to determine if they want to extend you credit. Depending on which creditor you talk to, they will want this number to be around20-30% (.2 to .3).

Please see Excel Appendix for how Excel can be used to calculate net worth.

Debt Payment Ratio – total monthly debt payments / after tax income

This ratio is one that banks look at as a measurement and assessment of your borrowing potential. You may also hear this called the debt to income ratio.

Savings Ratio – monthly savings / after tax income.

Aim for this number to be as high as you can because this means that you are doing your part in planning for emergencies and retirement.

Accredited Investing

At some point in your learning journey, you may hear someone ask you if you are an accredited investor. What this means that you would have earnings of $200,000 in the past two years or that you have $1 million in assets excluding the value of your primary residence (www.sec.gov). There are other stipulations for trust, business, banks, etc., but for an individual, these are the hurdles.

This is a rule that came out of the legislation following the Stock Market crash of 1929. Thus there are certain investments you will not be privy to if you do not meet these crucial rules. Whether we agree with the rule or not, this could end up being a goal of yours to meet the hurdles. At some point, if you are working your financial plan, you may meet this goal and be able to move on to other investment strategies.

L-Earning Prompts – Financial Statements

What are my financial ratios?

Do I consistently have more money going out than I have coming in?

Are my expenses evenly distributed to my flow of income?

Am I in a positive net worth scenario to be able to leave assets for heirs?

Is leaving assets for heirs important to me?

Why don't I experiment with an envelope system for a few months?

TAXES

Taxes can be intimidating because the tax code can be so lengthy and detailed. However, you can save a lot of tax preparation money by knowing how to handle your own tax preparation every year. Furthermore, sometimes you may need tax advice; you can handle learning aspects of this important area of your personal financial picture.

I have personally done my own taxes by hand, I have had a tax professional do them, and I have also completed my own taxes using software like TurboTax. Any way you want to do it is fine, but if you have a tax professional do it, be sure that you are clear on why you want someone else to do it. Avoid having someone else do your taxes just because you do not care to understand your taxes or you are afraid of making a mistake. Having a tax professional is great, but I quickly found out that my tax professional was waiting until the last minute to prepare mine, which put me in a bind for paying taxes one year. Plus, I really wanted a tax professional partner that would help me to understand tax strategies, or make recommendations on how to improve my tax situation.

Once I figured out that my tax professional was charging me over $600 for tax preparation without really helping me to have a different tax strategy, which is when I adopted TurboTax. TurboTax was so easy to use and prompted me for all of the information necessary, at a tenth of the price of the CPA, I was hooked.

The big boost for most on taxes is having home deductions or small business deductions – so that you can claim more than the standard deduction. Do not be afraid, as long as you are looking for tax deductions, rather than trying to commit tax evasion, you are ok in your learning journey. You want to take advantage of legitimate deductions, which is why they exist.

Also, giving is one of the ways that people can reduce taxes and this is a great habit to have in your financial plan. Again, you do not have to start out with huge dollars going to your favorite charity, but over time the amount you give could be substantial and save you taxes. Plus, if you want to ensure that heirs have access to money prior to your death, you can give money to family members up to a certain amount every year. Now this is not tax deductible for you, but it is tax free to the individual you are giving the money to – which can be very useful as a way of distributing your estate early if you choose.

L-Earning Prompts – Taxes

What are my deductions that I claim on my taxes?

What deductions can I claim on the 1040?

Do I know the deductions I can take advantage of?

What deductions am I curious about?

Do I have a habit of giving?

GOALS

In terms of financial goals, the more specific you are in stating your goal the higher the likelihood of success. For example, "I want to make more money this year" at least has a time frame specific boundary, but how much more do you want to make? A nickel more? Twenty percent more? And compared to what?

There are several components to goal setting that can help you be successful and this section outlines how to think about your personal financial goals. This section also includes strategies that you can try and see what works for you.

Celebrating Successes

Many years ago, I was listening to an interview of Jack Canfield and I do not remember what was being discussed on the interview but I do remember his suggestion of creating a list of your 100 greatest successes of your life. I decided to try this.

I gave this a try and I could write about a dozen successes, and got stuck. I put down things like I graduated from high school, I graduated from college, or I learned how to drive. These are the big things we think of in goal setting. But then it hit me like a ton of bricks – I also had many successes in achieving those goals, too. For example, I had finished kindergarten, I had finished first grade, and I had eventually learned how to calculate fractions which was a challenge for me. I started to see the steps along the way as successes just as much as the actual end goal.

All of a sudden, I started to feel very accomplished, in a way that I had never felt before. I started to see that success can happen in the smallest of activities, the smallest pieces that leverage you towards the accomplishment of a goal. From that moment on, I decided I would up the ante. I decided that it was important to track my successes through the year. To do this, I keep a calendar on me at all times and I write in it every day. It is for me to track my successes during the year and my goal is to have 100 successes at the end of each year.

In addition to this success list that I do annually, I also have an accountability partner that I celebrate those successes with after I have put the list together. I went to an event once where we would get standing ovations, sometimes for the smallest of things. As part of our practice, we had to, at least once, state that we deserved a standing ovation, just because, and everyone would stop what they were doing to give us the standing ovation. It was a practice in gratitude and acknowledgement that I have never forgotten. If there is one thing I believe, it is that you have to have an expansive consciousness when it comes to success. You cannot achieve as much as you want in a constricted or lacking mindset. In fact, to get the idea of how important this is, a good read is *Rich Dad, Poor Dad* by Robert Kiyosaki. He details very clearly how the contrast in thinking styles can help or hurt your chances of success.

Moving Goals Forward

How many times have you tried to set New Year's resolutions? It feels good to make these declarations, but how often do we achieve those resolutions? Only a small percentage of individuals are successful in achieving resolutions. Also, many people say that they have infrequent success in achieving resolutions. Finally, some people say that they never succeed and fail on their resolutions each year. Frankly, these are depressing pieces of information when it comes to goal achievement!

There can be many possible reasons for this. For example, making specific goals is important. So, if our goal is to "be happier" we have to be much more specific than that!

Secondly, one thing that can help is to have the feeling of movement towards a goal. So, when you set a goal, you want to make sure to set some action steps you can take this week. Create one action step that you absolutely with minimal effort can achieve. Create another action step that takes a little more engagement from you. This way, if the week gets away from you, then at a minimal you can achieve the minimal effort action step. This is huge for you psychologically – because you have to feel like you are moving forward.

Third, an important thing is to remember that you want to assess feedback on your goals at the same time. You can have a setback on a goal, and this is where managing your emotions are critical to your success. Feedback is feedback – but as you know so well, sometimes feedback feels good (like those lovely successes) but sometimes feedback can make us feel bad (like not being able to complete an action step or being told no).

However, if you can separate out the emotion and look at the situation objectively, you can ask yourself, what did I learn from this? How can I adjust my action step so that I can keep moving? Or even more importantly, do I need to adjust my goal in some way? Probably one of the most freeing things I ever learned was allowing myself to de-commit from a goal as I had originally stated it. Perhaps, just perhaps, as I learn through my action steps, I will find out that the goal really does not look like how I painted it originally.

Stopping Procrastination for Good

If you are a person that procrastinates, there is a sure way to deal with this that works. However, be very cautious with this, because it is a powerful strategy.

If you find that you really do want to achieve a goal, but you are having difficulty moving it forward, you may have to resort to the use of consequences. See, consequences can be positive – like when we celebrate our successes – that is a positive consequence! On the other end of this spectrum is when we have negative consequences.

Allow me to give an example. If I want to make sure that I achieve an action step, then I will make an agreement with my accountability partner that if I do not attempt this action step, then I will give up my iPad for a day or my laptop for a day. Trust me; I need to be connected to my devices, so to have one taken away would have a devastating effect on me and my work. Therefore, this provides the serious incentive and motivation I need to ensure that I take that action step.

Knowing When to Let Go

Sometimes we make goals and we achieve them. That is the perfect scenario. However, there are times when a goal seems to be elusive. Perhaps it means that the goal needs to be tweaked or perhaps you have not quite hit the nail on the head with specifics. Or, and this one may be difficult for some – you may need to abandon the goal altogether. Maybe the goal was never in alignment with your values, your true desires, or it does not fit your plan anymore. Know when to let go, because there is nothing worse than sticking to a goal that does not work for you, because that can become an emotional roadblock to actually working your plan over time.

Sharing Financial Responsibilities

Another wrinkle that needs to be considered in a financial plan is if you have children or other financial dependents. It is important to consider how you approach financial planning with other people in your life.

Some couples for instance like to share a checking account – yet this can have its challenges. What if someone does not like that you spend money on coffee every morning? What if someone thinks you are spending too much on a hobby? Sometimes, depending on the situation and the personalities involved, you may have a joint checking account for say "staple" expenses – like the electricity bill, the mortgage, etc. However, each person may need their own separate account for their own personal expenses, for the money spent that no one questions. Bottom line is this – you have to be able to express your expectations. And there is nothing wrong with experimenting with different approaches. Find what works for the dynamics of your relationship.

The financial dynamics with children can be equally tricky. It might be a good idea to have strategies for different ages. At what age would you want to start implementing an allowance? Will the child receive the allowance conditionally or unconditionally? Are your decisions about allowances aligned with what you would like for your children to learn about financial management? How much of your own personal financial situation will you reveal to them and at what age? What do you think your children are learning from you that you may not realize?

Children often live in reaction to their parents – they will mimic what you do, or they will reject what you do. Having open communications with them that are age appropriate is a real key to their development.

L-Earning Prompts – Goals

What are my goals?

Are my goals specific enough?

Am I flexible enough to be open to changing a goal or de-committing?

How do I ensure I do not drop the ball on a goal?

What is preventing me from setting goals?

How will I celebrate my achievements?

BASICS

There are certain basic necessities that everyone should have in order to have financial peace of mind. Remember, good habits will set you up for success, like paying yourself first. In addition, you want to have certain vigilance when it comes to monitoring your financial picture so that you can be proactive in protecting yourself and your financial future.

Furthermore, insurance is your hedge against disaster. Often a financial disaster can wipe you out for a while and cause much harm to your financial prospects for the future. Therefore, even though it can sometimes be tough to see those monthly dollars going out to pay for this hedge, when you need it, the financial affect can be a lot less devastating.

Emergency Fund

An emergency fund is an essential element of any financial plan. A general rule of thumb is to have at least six months of living expenses available for an emergency. Remember, this is an emergency fund, and you have to define what an emergency means. It can be as serious as you are in a car accident and cannot work for a little bit, or less serious like something occurred in your planning and you have to cover a gap in your cash flow. It is truly ok to handle emergencies like these with an emergency fund – however an emergency is not about buying a car that you could not afford otherwise. So make sure your emergency fund is in an account that is liquid, in other words, you can get access to this cash quickly if needed, but you have to have the discipline to not touch it unless it is an emergency. This could be a good place to define emergencies; you can always set up an accountability structure where you have to explain to someone why you want to take the money so that you have to convince them it is an emergency.

Be aware if your brain bets you up when you use an emergency fund. Remember, this is exactly why you have one. It is intended to help you pay for a deductible on a car repair or home repair or any other unexpected event. You want to avoid always using it for every day expenses, but for a true emergency where you need the cash to pay for something rather than always using a credit card, then you are fine (unless of course, you use a credit card for points, but with an emergency fund you have the cash to pay it off immediately).

Bank Reconciliations

We no longer have to actually get physical hard copies of bank statements from the bank. In Excel, since we can track this in our cash flow, all we have to do at any given date is to check the bank balance against what we are tracking our balance to be, and the difference is anything outstanding. In today's world of automatic withdrawals, we no longer have to wait for 2-3 days for checks to clear, but it is good to know if the bank balance you see at the ATM is the actual amount of money you have available.

Please see Excel Appendix for how Excel can be used to calculate your bank reconciliation.

Pay Yourself First

Paying yourself first can start small. Many advisors will tell you to pay yourself first by 10%. While this is a great goal, you may not be able to start out there. Start out with whatever you can afford to do, because the true goal is to establish a saving and investing habit. When possible, you want this automatic investing to occur on your paycheck without you having to think about it, because if you think about the investment then you may opt not to do it this month. This is why you want to take advantage of employee sponsored plans because once the setup is done you no longer have to make the decision to save or not to save.

Fraud and ID Theft

If you have never been the victim of bank fraud or identity theft, then be thankful for your blessings! One part of your game plan here is to have a good, reliable shredder or shredder scissors. This way, you know that nothing of your personal information is left behind. I even shred all of correspondence that has my mailing address on it.

One of the reasons I check my bank balance every day is because I was a victim of bank fraud and someone walked into a bank in another state and withdrew all of my available cash. I caught it right away, within a few hours of it occurring, and was able to proactively get the account frozen and open another bank account and start moving my direct deposits, automatic withdrawals, etc. Another good reason to have all of the websites, passwords, and other pertinent information all collected in one safe and secure place.

In addition, another good part of your plan is to have a relationship with your bank. I am notorious for using the online web access for the bank, however, it is good to go in periodically so that you are familiar with your local bank personnel and they are familiar with you. This way, you can also ask them about what other protections you can have on your accounts and explore ways of protecting yourself.

Finally, each of the credit reporting agencies (Transunion, Experian, and Equifax) gives you the ability to freeze your credit account if you have been a victim of identity theft. In most cases this is a free service, so bookmark those credit reporting agency websites on the pages where you can request a freeze on your credit and/or have the phone numbers of the agencies in your phone so that you can call to have this freeze placed on your account.

The best thing to do with your is to be knowledgeable about credit how to protect your credit. Take the steps now to learn about these sites and how they can help you keep your good credit rating at the highest level possible.

As a final note, in the age of computers, learn how to wipe your hard drive clean if you gift your computer to someone else after you are done with the machine. This applies to tablets as well. Most tablets and computers have a reset that can be done to get the device back to factory settings and wipe off all information on the device. Be sure you are familiar with how to do this is you are getting rid of an old device. Remember, our digital footprint is out there, and you are the guardian of that information.

Consumer Credit

Consumer credit comes in two important categories: secured and unsecured credit. Secured credit is something where you are paying off a balance over time, but there is an asset that backs up the credit. This type of credit applies to your home or car loans, because in the event you cannot repay the loan, the bank can repossess your car or home.

Unsecured credit is the type of credit we receive on a credit card. This type of credit does not have an asset that backs the credit. This type of credit we want to make sure is minimized. For example, a good rule of thumb is that if you have a credit card with a $10,000 credit limit then have no more than a $2,000 balance on it at any given time. It is better, if you can, that you charge something, but have the money to pay off the card right away, but if you have to carry a balance, make sure that it is 20% or less of the available credit line.

Credit Score

The three credit reporting agencies are required by law to allow you to receive one credit score report for free each year. I recommend staggering these three reports during the year. Of course, you can, if you want, get them all at the same time. If you get them all at the same time, or if you get one from Equifax in the first quarter of the year, then from Transunion in the second quarter of the year, etc., you will be able to proactively get incorrect information off of your credit report. There is also a good new service called Credit Karma, and this comes with an app for iPhone/Android and they have a lot of reading material about credit scores, etc. The credit score on this website, for you, is reported through Transunion and you can see the number as it changes over time and the service is completely free.

Buy and Insure a Car

For many of us a car is a necessity. Insuring the car is a must. So, whether you buy the car or lease the car, insurance is a must. Many variables can impact how much you pay in car insurance premiums. Plus, as you shop for a car to buy or lease, you can ask your agent for the amount of car insurance you may have to pay depending on what type of cars you are researching. Again, as a reminder, in our digital age, it may be easy for us to not go see our insurance agents, but getting to know them and asking them questions, we can easily start to see how they can help us to make good, sound financial decisions.

One thing you have to weigh when it comes to your cash flow forecast is the balance between deductibles and monthly insurance premiums. If you want to pay less each month, you can increase the deductibles. Be sure that you know the different deductible options and the corresponding insurance premium rates when you are deciding on insurance for your car.

Buy and Insure a House

Buying a house is probably one of the biggest investments a person can make in a lifetime. There are so many considerations to think about when thinking about buying versus renting. I was heavily influenced by my parents, like most of us, in deciding about home ownership. My parents rented for many years and did not buy a house until my father was in his fifties. I did not buy my first house until I was 49 years old. Besides the influence of my parents, there were a couple of other reasons I did not buy until that age.

One was because I was not sure where I wanted to have roots. For the longest time I did not feel tied to any one place. When I finally decided I wanted to be in one place, that helped set the stage for buying a house. Secondly, in most markets I have lived in, the rental prices were cheaper than buying a house. But once my rent started getting to the level of a mortgage, suddenly it did not seem to make sense to spend so much money for a non-asset.

Plus, no one had ever explained to me the tax advantages of having a house. For example, as a single person, my deductible was less than

$10,000, and when I got married, my deductible increased to $12,000. However, the interest in a mortgage can be substantial and is still an itemized deduction. Suddenly, I could deduct nearly $20,000 in mortgage interest and because of that; I could increase my deductions on my payroll so that I could take more home in each net paycheck.

Buying a house had other intangible rewards as well – such as, I was surprised at how much the idea of owning a home was daunting and could I handle repairs and all of the responsibility that came with a home, but once I decided I was going to live in a certain area of the country, the connection I had with that place was immeasurable and the pride of home ownership was unexpected in how powerfully positive that felt. It is a big responsibility to own a home, but the tax advantage it can give you can be substantial.

Health, Disability, and Life Insurance

Insurance was created to help a person avoid a major financial calamity. Health insurance is often provided by an employer, but we now have the option of also using the healthcare exchanges. Generally, insurance through an employer is a good way to go, and if you do not have that option, the exchanges are a good alternative for healthcare options. Generally, it is not a good idea to go without healthcare coverage, because if something happens, it could ruin you financially if you do not have any savings to cover a major event.

Disability coverage helps if you are ever disabled, and you can have coverage for a short-term event or a long-term event. For the most part, if these plans are offered by an employer they are relatively cheap. Even if your employer does not offer them, it is worth talking to some insurance carriers to find out your options.

Finally, basic term life insurance is often offered by employers. Many times they will provide basic life insurance equal to your salary for free, or at a small cost, and you can opt in for more coverage than that if you want to take advantage of it. There are many more types of insurance in the market place, things like variable life, whole life, etc. Some of these will pay cash benefits for certain life events or provide investments as part of the plan.

The types of insurances you obtain will depend largely on your needs. For example, if you have little kids, then this may be something where you want more life insurance coverage just in case something happens to you before the children reach the age of 18 or 21. Or, if you have not paid off your house, you may want to consider having enough coverage that in the event something happens to you, your spouse could pay off the house and continue to live in the house with lower expenses especially if the spouse is not a consistent wage earner.

L-Earning Prompts – Basics

Do I pay myself first? How do I pay myself first?

Do I want to buy a house?

How do rents and mortgages compare where I live?

Is this where I want to have roots?

Do I have an option for alternative transportation?

How do I want to handle the threats of theft and fraud?

What is my credit score?

Is there any negative information I need to correct on credit report(s)?

BUILDING WEALTH

Hopefully, over the course of one's life, you continuously build your wealth. Sometimes, other goals can get in the way, or disaster can strike, but remember, we want the habit of successful investing and saving over time and managing our emotions and thinking to stay as positive as we can. Again, the role of this book is to not tell you that saving for a child's education should come before your retirement – that decision is one you own. What I am saying is that regardless of the demands for your money, if you have a consistent habit of saving, have an emergency fund, and you keep your debts low, it will be much easier to maneuver these decisions over time.

I started out taking baby steps in investing. I first started a savings account and grew that to about $1000. I then started learning about certificates of deposit and started funneling money there for a bigger rate of return. Eventually, I started reading Money Magazine and immersed myself in learning about financial markets and various mutual fund strategies. As a learner, I wanted to read and digest as much information as I could and then take a calculated action.

Investing in Equities

Stocks are a very common investing platform for most of us. Most of us do not have the extra time bandwidth to spend a lot of time doing the analysis that it takes to pick our own stocks. This is why we will often invest in mutual funds or 401-k's and the like because there are professional fund managers out there that have the staff and the time to do the analysis. Thus, as a smart money manager, in this case, we can leverage off of other people and their expertise when it comes to picking stocks. Our role then becomes assessing if the fund's strategy is one that appeals to our risk profile.

For example, in my 401-k, I invest in a portfolio of equity funds and bond funds. Plus, within the equity funds, there can be all kinds of investment options. Each of them will have a prospectus that discusses the fund manager's approach to investing the money in the fund – read those carefully. Be sure you read them to figure out if you are in alignment with your risk tolerance and the investment strategy. For example, if your risk profile is one of a conservative, then you would perhaps not be interested in a venture capital fund, or you might want to restrict just how much you invest in a fund like that.

Regardless of what you decide, be sure to periodically review your investments in your 401-k and mutual funds to ensure that the funds are matching up with where you are in your life. In addition, how you invest at 20 years of age can be very different than how you invest at 50 years of age. Definitely, plan to review how you are investing your money.

At the very minimum, take advantage of employer sponsored 401-k plans. This is especially true if your plan offers matching funds. For example, an employer may have a plan where they match $1 for every $1 you invest in the 401-k, up to 5% of your pay. Here is how the math works:

If I make a gross salary of $50,000 and I invest the 5% maximum the employer will match, then I am investing $2,500 over a year. Based on the employer matching funds, then the employer will also match my $2,500 with another $2,500 if they match dollar for dollar. Regardless of where the market goes over that time frame, this is a nice return on my money.

In addition, pay attention to the rules of vesting, because some companies will make you wait before these matching funds become yours while other companies will have them vest immediately; so check your vesting rules so that you are aware of when those matching funds become your money that you can touch for your retirement.

Finally, some companies will offer discounts on buying company stock and this can be useful in your financial plan, too. However, be sure to become knowledgeable about your company financial performance BEYOND what your leaders say. Learn how to do your own analysis of the company financial performance and read different views about the company from a financial perspective. For instance, the Apple iPhone has a stock tracker that is tied to yahoo finance and I have some stock that I invest in personally listed there so that I can read financial news about the company at any time. Therefore, I keep a finger on the pulse of the stock market and specific stocks that I directly invest in. In addition, I can read a financial statement and perform my own ratio analysis.

Investing in Debt

We are used to investing in equity, but you also have the option to invest in debt. Meaning, you can invest in loans that are given to other people – a type of crowd funding. To illustrate an example of this take a look at www.lendingclub.com. What happens with this site is that individuals request to borrow money. Lending club will review the credit history and approve whether or not the person can borrow the amount of money they desire, plus, depending on their credit history, the person may be deemed as "A" borrower, meaning they have good credit and will be charged a lower amount of interest for the loan. On the other hand, the person may be rated a "B" or "C" or lower borrower, meaning that they have less than stellar credit and will be charged a higher amount of interest.

Then, investors like me come along and maybe I have $100 to invest, and many others have $100 to invest, then we pool all our money together through the site to fund the person's loan. Then what happens is over the life of the loan, we share in the interest charged to the borrower. Therefore, on an "A" loan we earn less interest maybe 4-6%, but it would still be more than what we can earn at a bank on a savings account. Ultimately, you would invest in a mixture of loan grades, maybe more of them in the "A" and "B" categories with a few "C", and "D" loans in order to earn a higher interest rate.

The important thing to realize here is that you want to have diversification. Meaning, have a goal to not have all your retirement dollars in only equities (stocks) because this puts you at risk. Investing in debt can earn you a very steady interest rate that is much better than a certificate of deposit or a savings account.

Other Investing

As your learning deepens on financial planning, you may get to the point where you will want to open your own brokerage account. A brokerage account allows you to invest directly in different company stocks (not just the company that you work for, for example). There are many brokerage companies out there, and they will charge various different commission rates, but the most important thing to look for is the tools the brokerage company offers you to learn. One of the things you must look for is a virtual trading platform – a good example of this is www.optionsxpress.com. This brokerage company has a virtual trading platform that allows you to practice investing with virtual money, but the results are tied to the actual stock market. Therefore, you can take $10,000 virtual dollars and invest in companies like Google, Apple, Disney, or any other company you are interested in. This allows you to see how it feels when the market moves in one direction or the other and allows you to work through the emotions of investing without using your own money.

This is especially important if you ever get interested in trading options. As you learn the techniques of trading options, being able to do this with virtual money is essential to your long-term success.

Basic Overview of Options

This section is not intended to be a full explanation of options. This section is intended to give you an idea of how useful they can be as an additional strategy.

There are many sources for option information; however, I learned these strategies from Dr Stephen Cooper at www.onlineoptions.com. There are plenty of resources out there, so if you are interested in this as an investing strategy, ask friends, look for recommendations, because you have to work with who you are comfortable with.

What are Options

Options are a derivative. Basically what that means is that the value of the derivative is driven by something else. In this case, stock options are a contract that gets their value from the underlying stock.

Any company that is traded could have options, and many of them do. Most companies you can think of have options like Starbucks, Microsoft, Southwest Airlines, Google, Apple, etc. What is nice is that many of us cannot invest in a company like Google because of the stock price – that company has seen stock prices as high as $1,000. However, the option could be as cheap as $100 or less, depending on your strategy you want to employ. This gives you more leverage.

The price of options will move with the price of the underlying stock and based on other factors, such as the time remaining before the option expires. Your goal is to take advantage of the price movements and to understand how to do that. Therefore, I will first explain some terminology and then go through a couple of examples of this strategy.

Options Terminology

Option – the underlying derivative of a stock. Example, Southwest Airlines trades its stock as LUV (the ticker symbol) and they have all kinds of options available. To see this, go to finance.yahoo.com. In the quote lookup entry box, type "LUV". You will then see information about the underlying stock of Southwest Airlines. On the left hand side of the page will be a list of links, so click on "Options". Here you will see the various pieces of information.

Strike Price - there will be all kinds of strike prices. For example if Southwest Airlines is currently trading at $20.55, there can be strike prices of $18, $19, $20, $21, $22, etc.

Call Options – Call options are contracts that investors buy and sell if they expect the market to go higher.

Put Options – Put options are contracts that investors buy and sell if they expect the market to go lower.

Expiration – Across the top are expiration months. Each contract has a month and year that they will expire. Yahoo finance will also tell you the day of the month that the options will expire (it is the third Friday of any month) and the official market close out occurs on Saturday.

Option Symbol – Each option has its own symbol which includes the underlying stock ticker symbol, the two digit year, the two digit month, and the two digit day, "C" for call or "P" for Put, and the strike price of the option.

Bid Price – Bid prices are the max price buyers are willing to pay.

Ask Price – Ask prices are the min prices the sellers are willing to receive.

Volume – The volume represents how many of the options have been transacted on this day.

Open Interest – This represents open contracts that have not been closed.

Options Example 1: Covered Calls

Continuing to use Southwest Airlines as an example, consider the following scenario: Assume the price of Southwest Airlines stock is $20.15 and you purchase 100 shares. You have spent $2,015 plus a commission.

As long as you own 100 shares of a stock, and you have basic options trading approval in your brokerage account, then you can SELL calls to other investors. So, how does this help you?

When you own 100 shares, you can sell one call contract (one contract represents 100 underlying shares). You can sell this contract, and let's say that the price you sell it for is .35 cents (this means, you receive in your brokerage account .35 cents times 100 underlying shares – so you have now received cash on the sale of $35. The contract may expire in say 20 days. In those 20 days, the idea is that more often than not, this contract would expire worthless, that the investor who bought your call would not exercise the option and buy your shares.

Therefore, if the contract expires, you now have earned $35 in a twenty day period. As a return percentage this equates to 1.74% ($35 / $2,015.

Remember, in this case the value is assumed to be the original purchase price; and, as a yearly rate of return, in a year, you have 18.25 twenty day periods. So your annual rate of return is 1.74% times 18.25 which equals 31.76% rate of return. What bank can beat that as a return?

But what if the contract is executed and your shares are bought out from under you? Well, you will end up with the following in this scenario:

You would still earn the percentage already calculated on the sale of the call contract, but you will also earn a profit on the difference between the strike price of $21 and the purchase price of $20.15. Thus, you will also generate more cash in your account of $21-$20.15 = .45 cents times 100 shares = $45. Depending on how long you owned the underlying shares, you can have a very decent annual return there too!

There are many considerations in doing a covered call strategy – so please do know that more research and learning must take place for any individual investor to do this strategy well, but you can learn it and you can do it!

Options Example 2: Buying Calls

In addition, you can buy calls and this is an appropriate strategy if you feel that the underlying stock value is going to continue to rise. There are ways to examine an underlying stock and choosing the underlying stock which I won't go into here. Remember, any strategy requires some research and some practice on a virtual trading platform (and many brokerages teach webinars on these strategies).

Here is how this works….in this example I will use Starbucks as an example. For instance, you could buy a call that will expire in say three months and the price of the call is $2, thus you will spend $200 plus a commission. The underlying stock price could be say $70.

Since the contract will expire in three months, you want to look to close out this position at least one month before the expiration (because at that time the option will definitely start losing value rapidly). So you essentially will have about 60 days for the underlying stock to keep going up. As long as it does, then let's say that within 30 days, the option has gone up to $2.50 for that contract. We will also assume that we will close out that position at that 30 day mark.

How much have you made? You originally spent $200; you closed out the position for $250 (I am not including the commissions in the calculations). You have made $50 and that is a 25% return in thirty days ($50 / $200). In a year, there are 12.17 thirty day periods. Thus you have earned an annual return of a whopping 304%.

Summary

As you can see, there are so many ways to earn money and there are several keys to your success. One, keep learning no matter what. Two, stay curious about different investments. Three, take as long as you need to learn and feel comfortable with any investing strategy, practice virtually if you can, and then have fun with your l-earning journey.

There is nothing more empowering than knowing all kinds of strategies that cover all manner of investments. Your financial plan can be exciting and interesting and I hope that this has whet your appetite for how cool it can be to l-earn.

L-Earning Prompts – Building Wealth

What is my risk profile or risk tolerance?

What am I comfortable investing in?

What investment ideas do I want to know more about?

How do I handle my emotions as I learn?

How do I handle my emotions if I have a loss?

Are my investment choices consistent with my risk tolerance?

Have I diversified across my portfolio?

Am I investing in a mix of stocks, bonds, and debt?

PRESERVING WEALTH

Over the lifetime of any person, the best laid plans can go awry. You will likely find that personal financial planning will have peaks and valleys. The key over time is to keep your emotions in check and to stay open to learning.

In your twenties, you are just starting out likely in your first job after college. Some of you may start working full time directly out of high school. Either way, learn about different investment tools, know what the company you work for offers, and get started with what you are comfortable with so that you can get a head start.

In your twenties to thirties, you may start having children, or you may even buy your first house. Do not worry if sometimes other financial demands keep you from investing huge amounts of money, but regardless of what else you may do, keep investing in your retirement. Remember, the real key to long term success is to keep the good investing habit going at all times.

Your forties and fifties will be your peak earning years. You want to set yourself up in these years to be stocking away as much money as you possibly can. It is during this time of your life that you want to be on target for your retirement funds. The big key is to have diversification, not only within your portfolio in the stock market, but also be invested in bonds, debt instruments, and various other kinds of investments.

By the time you are in your sixties and seventies, you will be finalizing your retirement plans. This will include whether or not you will be attempting to continue to work or not, where exactly you will retire geographically, and how much social security will be a part of your overall plan. Many people have predicted the demise of social security. As I plan, I try to not put too much weight on social security, and what I mean by this is I want to be in charge of my own destiny, which regardless of what happens with social security, I can still retire on my terms. My gut tells me that perhaps social security will be still in its current form, but will pay out less to retirees, OR, that social security may become privatized, meaning that you can direct your own funds. Either way, I personally do not believe it will cease to exist, but I have no evidence one way or the other. No one can predict the future. Therefore, the big key for any of us is to be proactive, be willing to learn, and direct your financial planning partners (CPA's, insurance agents, and investment advisors). Period. You are the controller.

Retirement

Retirement funding is important to consider throughout the lifetime of a person, and please do everything you can to not wait to the last minute to address this important financial goal. Do not get caught in your sixties fifties or sixties attempting to fund retirement. At this point, you could be woefully behind if you have not been paying attention to this important lifelong plan.

Financial advisors often have sophisticated projection software to project out how much you will have in retirement funds based on current savings habits and how many years you have left until retirement. Or you can find these kinds of templates on the Internet. However, I can project out my retirement savings, too, using Excel and over time that is exactly what I have done. I can make certain assumptions about interest rates, gains, market fluctuations, etc., and get my own idea of how well I am doing through time. Whichever way you decide to do this is fine, just know that if you rely on a professional to do this for you, you will likely end up paying for the service. Over time you will figure out what you like to do to stay in control of your own plan.

Social Security

At the following website, www.ssa.gov/myaccount you can set up an account and be able to see your projected social security benefits based on various life events. On this website you can also see your lifetime earnings and various pieces of other information. This is a great way to keep tabs on changes in social security. You can get this same information in the mail, but for security reasons I prefer to find the information through the social security administration website. You can also see the full retirement age, your benefits if you retire early or later than that age.

Estate Planning

Your estate, once you are gone, can be a burden for those left behind, or not, based on the choices you make in planning for the distribution of your assets. Remember when we discussed the net worth statement? This is a key element in planning what will happen with your estate. If you want to leave something for those who survive you, then it is important to have more assets than you have debt. In addition, the various documents you can have for your estate can keep your heirs from having to pay probate costs or taxes on assets that are to transfer ownership. Learning about the documents is crucial to not only your peace of mind but for those people you remain after you are gone. If you, or your family, have difficulty discussing this morbid topic, examine why that is. It is important to have the conversations before it is too late.

Will

The will establishes what your wishes are regarding your estate. This document names your executor, the person that will carry out your wishes, which can be a family member, but can also be a representative of a bank (which might be good for the sake of conflicts of interest). Another important element on a will is to identify what will happen to minor children.

Powers of Attorney

This document allows you to name a person that can handle your affairs in case you are not able to do it yourself while you are still alive. An example would be, who can manage your affairs if you were to be in a coma and therefore not able to write checks and otherwise handle your affairs. The documents can cover not only financial matters but who can make decisions for you on health care too, in case you cannot do it yourself. Be sure this is someone you trust and completely understands your desires.

Revocable Living Trust

This document allows for the smooth transfer of property and thus avoiding probate court fees. The trust must "own" all of your property and this can be a challenge to maintain. Therefore, start building a good relationship with your legal representative to know exactly what is required so that you can take advantage of these document's powerful features.

Advanced Directive

You may also see this discussed as a living will. This document will direct a doctor to continue to have you on life support or to pull the plug. Make sure your wishes are in place and that your power of attorney knows that you have these documents and where they are in case they are needed.

L-Earning Prompts – Preserving Wealth

Do I have all of the necessary financial documents?

Will my dependents be in a financial bind if I died today?

What happens to minor children in the event I died today?

Do I have adequate retirement planning?

Do I know my social security projected benefits?

What is my idea of retirement? Same lifestyle? Different lifestyle?

What are realistic expense expectations in my retirement?

PUTTING IT TOGETHER

The entire book is a financial plan. If you go through each section and walk through the prompts and consider the information contained in each section, you can write your own financial plan. Words of caution – do not worry how long it takes you to put together a plan. Unless you have some sort of urgency, like you already know that you have a terminal condition, or that retirement is a month away, you have time to put this together. Take your time. Set goals to get through one section at a time.

All along the way, you will have situations occur that teach you – do not worry if they feel good or they feel bad. Learn from ALL of the experiences. Emotions are pieces of information, just like numbers on a piece of paper, or the news on the TV. Emotions are pieces of data that you can analyze and understand in order to help you achieve your goals. To avoid feelings is to avoid l-earning.

Finally, be flexible. Conditions can change. Roll with those punches as they come. You will find a rhythm that works for you. You will know when to review your plan, when to make changes, and when you may need to find more resources. Be willing to create new goal, change a goal, or fully de-commit from something that is not working for you. You own it.

It may feel overwhelming right now, because it is a lot of information to digest, but you will get the hang of it and remember this is about your development over time as the chief financial officer of your financial portfolio and your financial team. You are in charge and learning to trust your leadership is what it is all about. Enjoy the l-earning!

RECOMMENDED RESOURCES

Rich Dad, Poor Dad, by Robert Kiyosaki

The Richest Man in Babylon, George Samuel Clason

How We Decide, Jonah Lehrer

Money Magazine

Excuse Me, Your Life is Waiting, Lynn Grabhorn

Change Your Questions Change Your Life, Marilee Adams

EXCEL APPENDIX

Excel: Setting Password

The notes are using Microsoft Excel 2010. No matter what version you are using, you can press the F1 key for the help function. For example, if you have a different version you can look up something like "password protection" and find the instructions for how to do this in your specific version.

First, open up Excel, and name your file. Click on ***File, Save*** and name your file. Even though we have not developed the spreadsheet, you will have the file ready for changes.

Now, I will show you how to put a password on the file. Click ***File***, and then click on ***Save As***. You will see this screen:

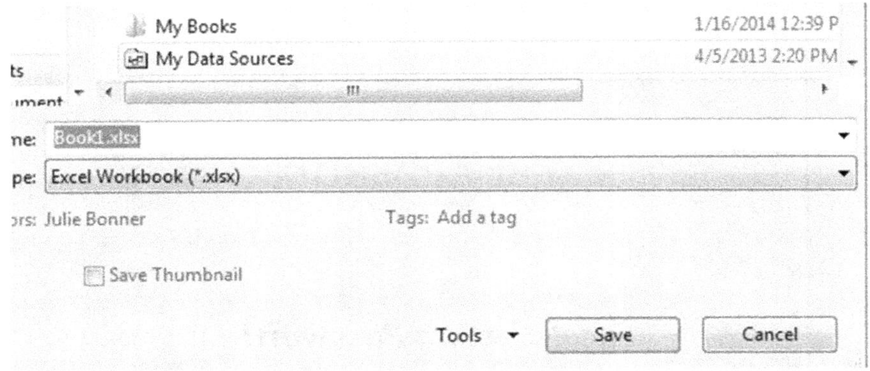

Click on ***Tools*** and then click on ***General Options*** and then you will see the following dialogue box:

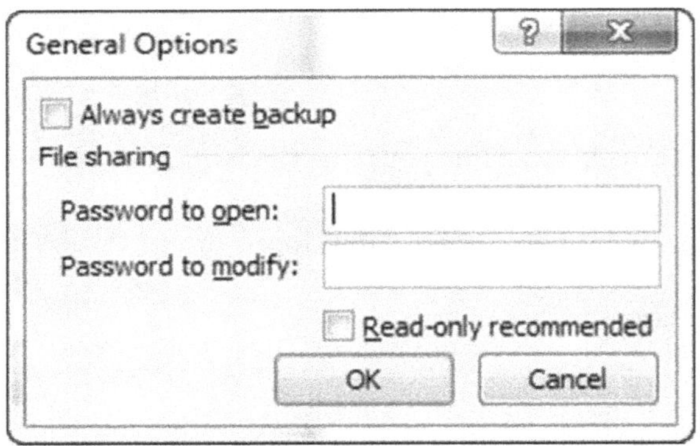

The field called ***Password to open:*** is the password that you would have to type in to open the file. If you only set this password, then a person has to know the password to open and modify the file. It is best to set it like this, because if you put in a ***Password to modify:*** then a person can open a read only copy of your file. If you have sensitive information like PINs, passwords, and your social security numnber stored in there than anyone could read it and steal your identity. The click ***OK***. Then click ***Save***.

Excel: Setting Up Tab Names

In an Excel file you may have several tabs that are linked together – since you will be tracking so many different things in your financial life. Therefore, you may want to give descriptive names to the tabs. In a normal Excel file, you will only see the following:

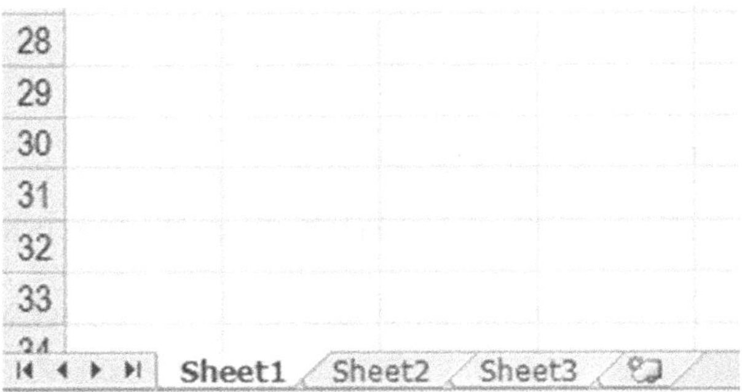

You can change the ***Sheet1*** to a more descriptive name. We will assume you want to call it "Cash Flow", so here is how to change it.

Right click on the tab called Sheet1. Choose ***Rename***. The letters on Sheet1 will then be highlighted and you can change it to "Cash Flow" – so now the tab will look like this:

Excel: Setting Up Weekdays

In cell C1, type the text *MON* (for Monday).

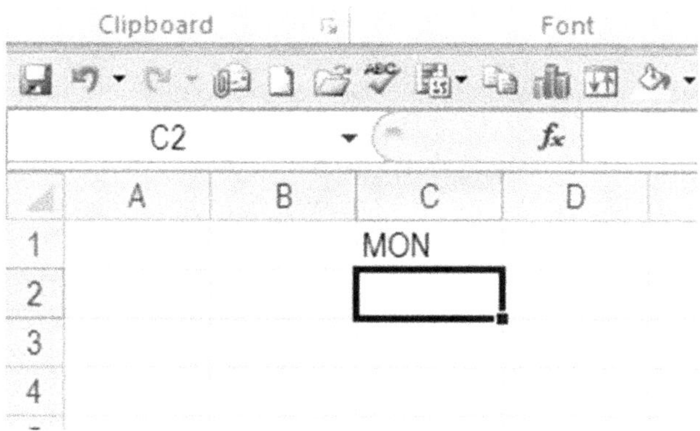

Now, click on cell C1, and the the lower right hand corner, if you hover the cursor over that corner, the cursor will change to a small black cross. Once you see that, you can click and drag to the right – Excel will automatically fill in ***Tue, Wed, Thu, etc.***

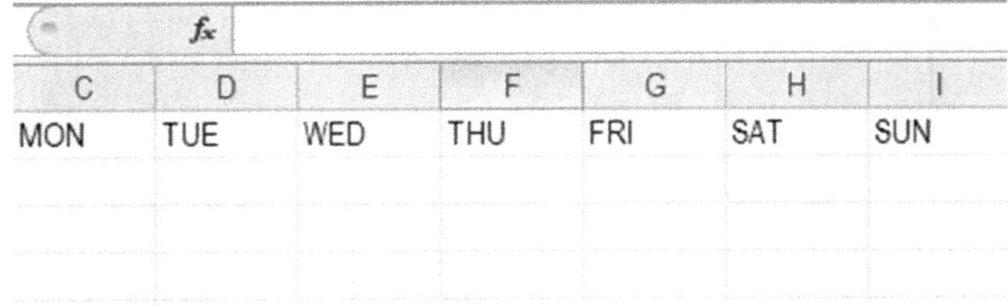

Excel: Setting Up Cash Flow

In cell C2, you can type the date (assuming that Monday is 2/17/14). Type the date as 2/17/14. And depending on how you want the date to look, you can change the format by going to *Home* page and click in the area where you see the number formats.

Once you have decided on the date format, you can create a formula for the others dates. In cell D2, type the formula exactly as you see it here:

=C2+1

Press the Enter key

In cell D2, you will now see the entry 2/18/14.

Now, when you click on cell D2, you can hover the mouse over the right hand lower corner of the cell, watch the cursor turn into the short black cross, click on the corner and drag it across. Excel will then fill in all of the dates, based on your formula. Now you will have the following set up:

C	D	E	F	G	H	I
MON	TUE	WED	THU	FRI	SAT	SUN
2/17/2014	2/18/2014	2/19/2014	2/20/2014	2/21/2014	2/22/2014	2/23/2014

Excel: Setting Cash Flow Categories

Now, in cell B3, you will set the beginning balance of your bank account. We will assume it to be $2,200. See the screenshot:

B	C	D	E	F	G	H
	MON	TUE	WED	THU	FRI	SAT
	2/17/2014	2/18/2014	2/19/2014	2/20/2014	2/21/2014	2/22/2014
Beg Bal	2200					

Now start entering your income and expense categories in Cell B4. You can name them whatever you would like, this is just a sample:

B	C	D	E
	MON	TUE	WED
	2/17/2014	2/18/2014	2/19/2014
Beg Bal	2200		
Income			
Mortgage			
Water			
Car			
Electricity			
Cable			

Eventually, you will want an ending balance heading, like this:

B	C	D	E
	MON	TUE	WED
	2/17/2014	2/18/2014	2/19/2014
Beg Bal	2200		
Income			
Mortgage			
Water			
Car			
Electricity			
Cable			
End Bal			

Make sure there is a blank line between the last expense category just in case you have to add more later.

In the cell next to the “End Bal”, you will set a formula. Click on the cell nest to “End Bal” and then click on this icon in the upper right hand menu:

When you click on the auto sum icon, Excel will set a formula that highlights the cell you are in all the way up to the 2200 beginning balance. Click Enter, and you will see the following:

=SUM(C3:C10)

B	C	D	E	
	MON	TUE	WED	T
	2/17/2014	2/18/2014	2/19/2014	2
Beg Bal	2200			
Income				
Mortgage				
Water				
Car				
Electricity				
Cable				
End Bal	2200			

Now, you can click on the cell next to “End Bal”, hover the mouse over the loawer right hand corner, wait for the cursor to turn into the short black cross, click on that and drag the formala across. Now the sheet will look like this:

	MON	TUE	WED	THU	FRI	SAT	SUN
	2/17/2014	2/18/2014	2/19/2014	2/20/2014	2/21/2014	2/22/2014	2/23/2014
Beg Bal	2200						
Income							
Mortgage							
Water							
Car							
Electricity							
Cable							
End Bal	2200	0	0	0	0	0	0

In the cell underneath the cell that has “2/18/14”, you want to add a formula. In that cell you want to click the = sign, and then click on the ending balance cell under “2/17/14” and click enter. Now that cell will look like this:

fx =+C11

B	C	D	E	F	G
	MON	TUE	WED	THU	FRI
	2/17/2014	2/18/2014	2/19/2014	2/20/2014	2/21/2014
Beg Bal	2200	2200	2200	2200	2200
Income					
Mortgage					
Water					
Car					
Electricity					
Cable					
End Bal	2200	2200	2200	2200	2200

Now, click on the cell right below "2/18/14", hover the lower right hand corner, wait for the cursor to turn into the short black cross, click on it and drag it across. Now the week will look like this:

B	C	D	E	F	G	H	I
	MON	TUE	WED	THU	FRI	SAT	SUN
	2/17/2014	2/18/2014	2/19/2014	2/20/2014	2/21/2014	2/22/2014	2/23/2014
Beg Bal	2200	2200	2200	2200	2200	2200	2200
Income							
Mortgage							
Water							
Car							
Electricity							
Cable							
End Bal	2200	2200	2200	2200	2200	2200	2200

Now, if your water bill is due on the 19th, you can enter the amount. Maybe you know the exact amount or perhaps it can vary from month to month. Whatever number, you enter in the field for the 19th, for the water bill, you will enter it as a negative number – thus, enter a minus sign in front of it. Let's assume the water bill averages $100 a month. Now that you have entered it, the sheet will look like this:

B	C	D	E	F	G
	MON	TUE	WED	THU	FRI
	2/17/2014	2/18/2014	2/19/2014	2/20/2014	2/21/2014
Beg Bal	2200	2200	2200	2100	2100
Income					
Mortgage					
Water			-100		
Car					
Electricity					
Cable					
End Bal	2200	2200	2100	2100	2100

Notice that one we entered the deduction of the expense, the rest of the formulas changed accordingly.

Now assume income comes in on Friday, and the amount is $800. Then enter that as a positve number and notice the change in your sheet:

B	C	D	E	F	G
	MON	TUE	WED	THU	FRI
	2/17/2014	2/18/2014	2/19/2014	2/20/2014	2/21/2014
Beg Bal	2200	2200	2200	2100	2100
Income					800
Mortgage					
Water			-100		
Car					
Electricity					
Cable					
End Bal	2200	2200	2100	2100	2900

Now you can start entering in the rest of your expenses, and expand out the calendar for as long as you want. I typically at least go forward for 90 days.

These are the basics and depending on other things you want to see or calculate, our learning community can assist on Facebook. Please connect at jrbonner10@gmail.com and request to be added to the "Lifelong L-Earning" community.

Excel: Setting Up Bank Reconciliation

Now we will set another tab to be the "Bank Recon" tab. You set it up exactly like we set up the renamed "Cash Flow" tab:

Here we can quickly and easily reconcile the information at your bank, compared to your running balance in your spreadsheet.

Now, on this tab, in Cell A2, type the text: "Bank Bal". Underneath that cell, type the text "My Bal". Let us assume, that today in 2/19/14. We have written the check or submitted the withdrawal for the water bill. Assuming that the bank balance is $2,200 and fo course, according to our balance for 2/19/14, my balance is $2,100 (Assuming the amount for the water bill was exactlyt $100).

In the cell next to “Bank Bal” type $2,200, and in the cell next to “My Bal” type in $2,100. Type the text “Difference” underneath “My Bal”. Now enter in a formula next to the “Difference” cell that is = the “Bank Bal” minus the “My Bal”. The tab now looks like this:

B8 fx

	A	B	C	D
1				
2	Bank Bal	2200		
3	My Bal	2100		
4	Difference	100		
5				
6				

Now, below the “Difference” cell, we will list the outstanding items.

Then, the sheet looks like this:

G9 | f_x

	A	B	C	D
1				
2	Bank Bal	2200		
3	My Bal	2100		
4	Difference	100		
5	Water Bill	100		
6				
7				
8				
9				

Now, we will add a "Net" text a few rows below (and leave some blanks so you can have room for other outstanding items). And I am showing in the screen shot below what the formula would look like:

B8 | f_x | =+B4-SUM(B5:B7)

	A	B	C	D	E
1					
2	Bank Bal	2200			
3	My Bal	2100			
4	Difference	100			
5	Water Bill	100			
6					
7					
8	Net	0			

Thus, this formula is taking B4 which is the difference of $100, and substracting from it the sum of the cells B5 through B7 added together.

Excel: Setting Up Net Worth

We will now set up the net worth tab. Change another tab name to be "Net Worth". In cell B2, we will type the text "Assets". Then from that cell, highlight four cells across by using the SHIFT + the right arrow key. The sheet will look like this:

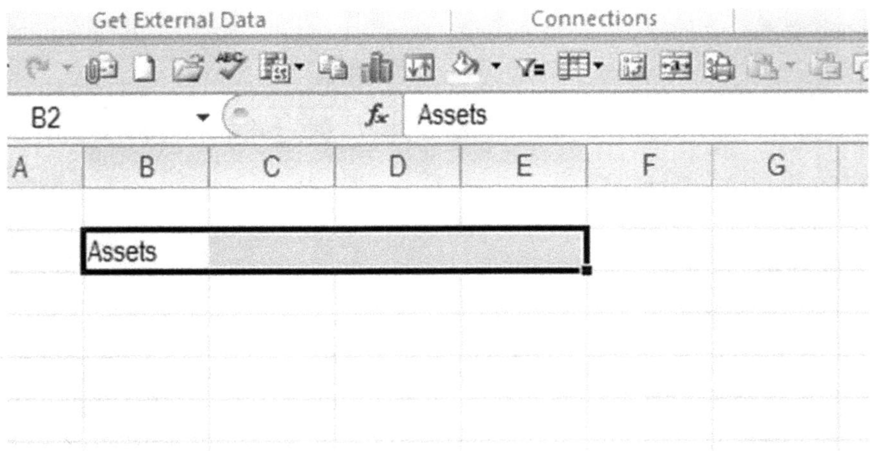

Now, on the HOME tab, click on the "Merge & Center" icon:

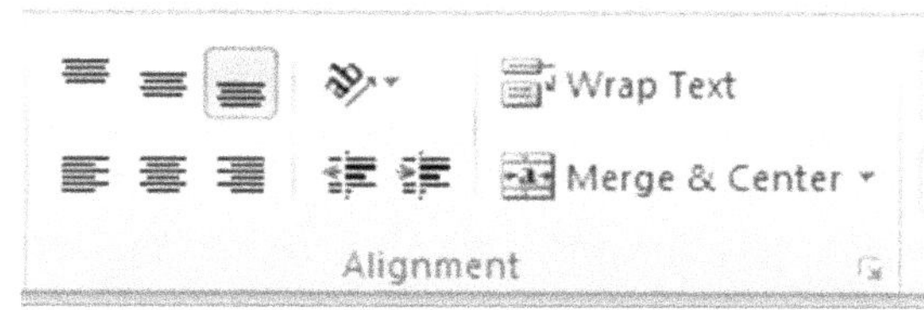

Now the word "Assets" will center across the four cells like this:

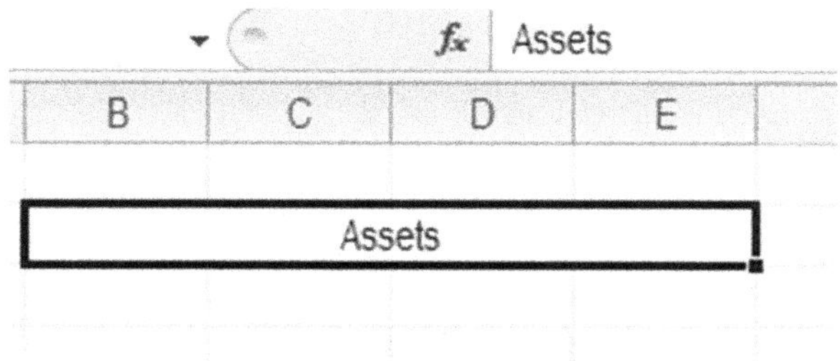

Now we start listing the assets. The first one will be your bank checking account. Now you can add other text to have the sheet look like this:

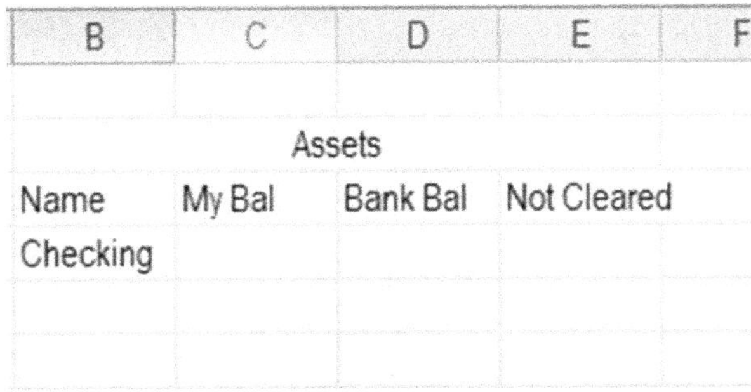

Now we can set a formula that hooks into another tab. The "My Bal" number is going to come from the "Bank Recon" tab. You enter the formula with the equals sign and then click over to the "Bank Recon" tab and click on the "My Bal" cell that contains the dollars. This screen shot shows how this will look along with the formula:

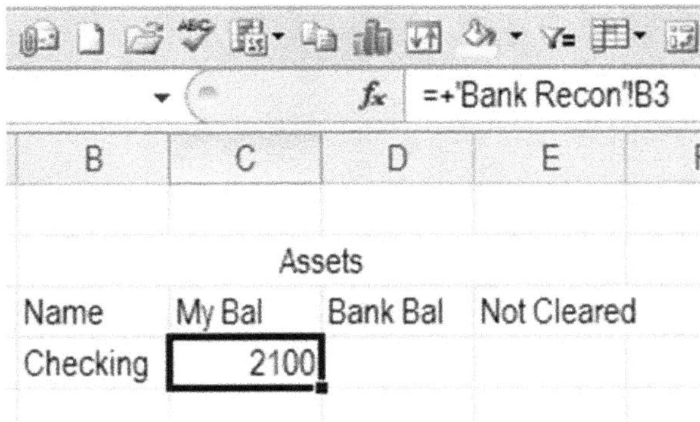

Do the same this with the "Bank Bal" and the "Not Cleared" columns.

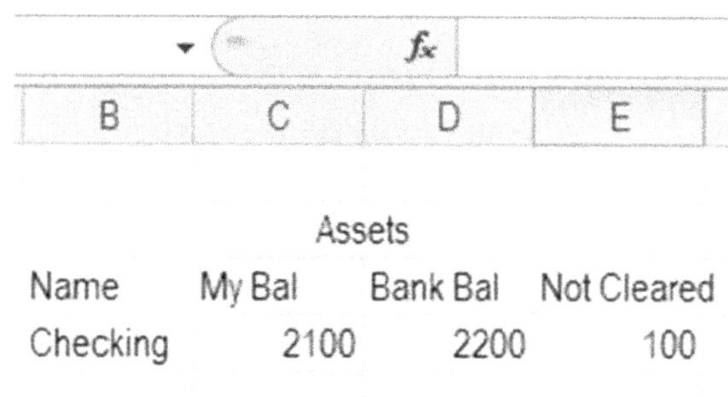

B	C	D	E
	Assets		
Name	My Bal	Bank Bal	Not Cleared
Checking	2100	2200	100

Now, you can list other assets. If you have a house, then the value of the last appraisal. We can assume in this example that we own a house and the last appraisal was $350,000.

Now the spreadsheet looks like this:

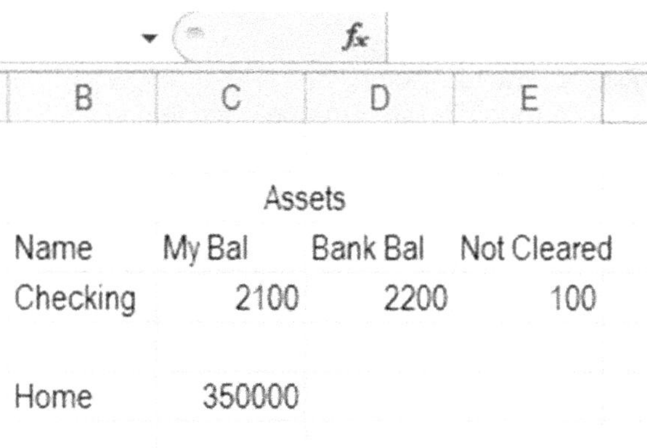

B	C	D	E
	Assets		
Name	My Bal	Bank Bal	Not Cleared
Checking	2100	2200	100
Home	350000		

We also have a car, and the blue book value of it is $6,000. We add up all our assets, with the autosum tool I showed you previously. Now this tabe looks like this:

B	C	D	E
	Assets		
Name	My Bal	Bank Bal	Not Cleared
Checking	2100	2200	100
Home	350000		
Car	6000		
Total	358100		

In the future any changes in the bank balance will automatically update here, but if we get a new appraisal, then you have to enter that, or if the blue book value changes, you will have to manually change the value.

Now you add in the liabilities, just like the assets. We can assume we have a tiny bit left of a loan on the car, and we have a loan still outstanding with the home, and we have one credit card with a balance on it. The "Due" column represents our minimum due or the contractual amount we owe each month – on most loans we can prepay on the principal, so do that when you can. Then add the total of your liabilities with the autosum function, and then create a formula that take the total assets and subtracts the total liabilities. You can see that formula on the screenshot below:

B	C	D	E	F	G	H	I
	Assets					Liabilities	
Name	My Bal	Bank Bal	Not Cleared		Name	Due	Balance
Checking	2100	2200	100				
Home	350000				Home	2000	250000
Car	6000				Car	200	2000
					Credit Card	25	1500
Total	358100				Total		253500
					Net Worth		104600

Excel: Setting Up Stock Tracking

One of the other assets you may list is your 401-k, or other stock related investments. You can set up a tab that tracks the stocks you own. We will create another tab called "Stocks", but of course, you can name it anything that fits your purpose. Now we have four tabs:

Now, go to the "Stocks" tab, and then click on the "Data" menu on the top of the Excel ribbon:

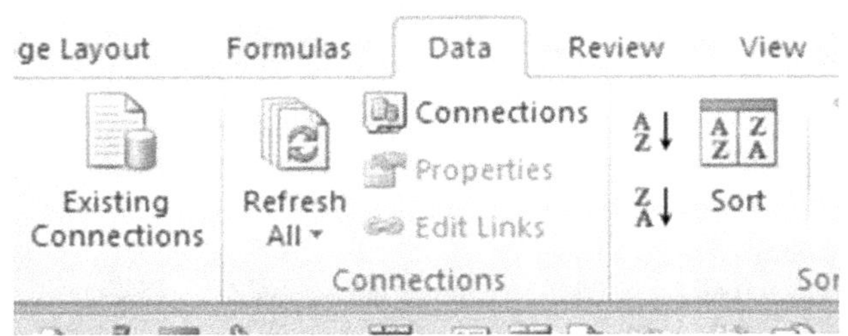

Clcik on "Existing Connections" and you will see:

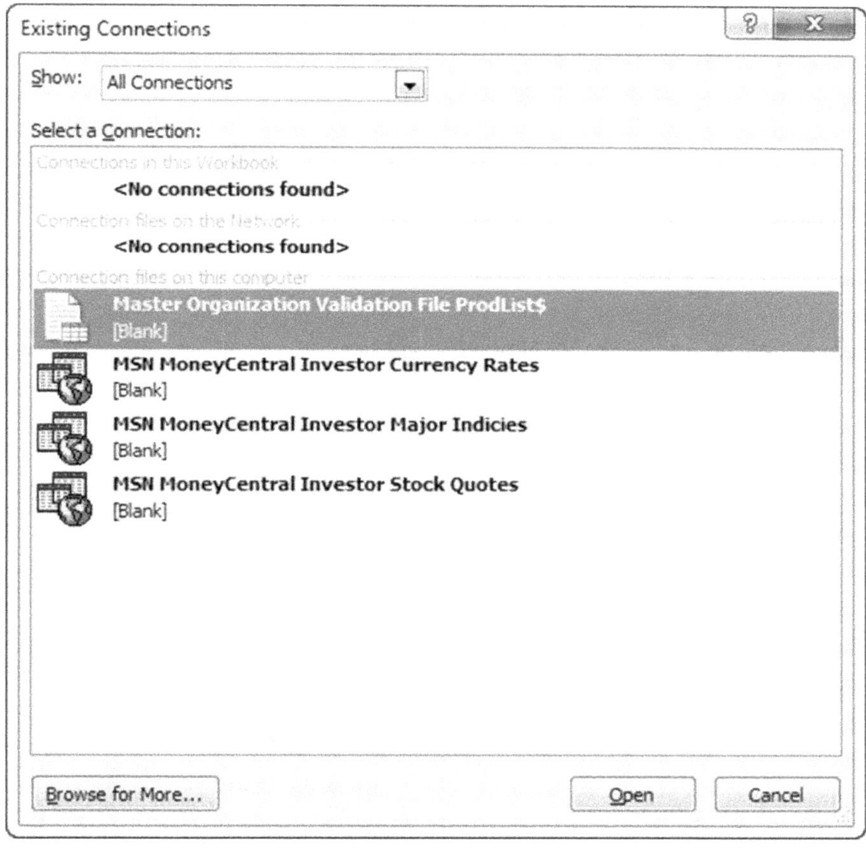

Click on "MSN MoneyCentral Investor Stock Quotes" and click "Open" – you will see this dialogue box:

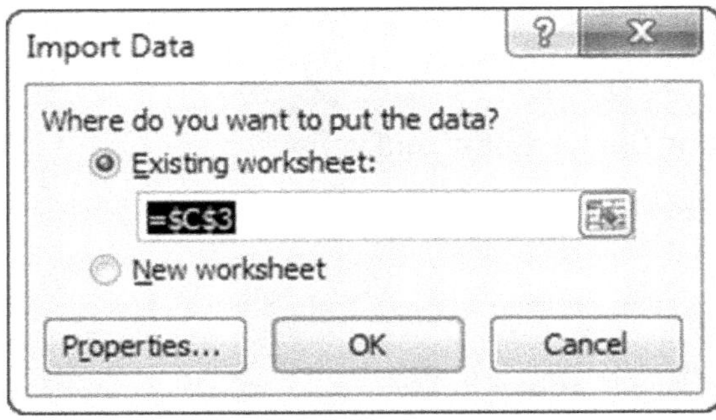

If you want the data we pull to start in cell C3, then click OK or if you want to change the cell you can do so in this dialogue box. I am going to leave it alone and click OK. Now you will see:

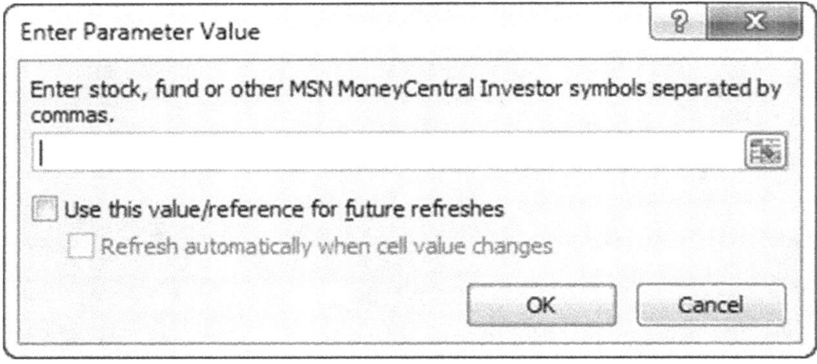

Here I will enter four stock symbols, SBUX for Starbucks, GOOG for Google, LUV for Southwest Airlines, and COST for Costco. The dialogue box will look like this:

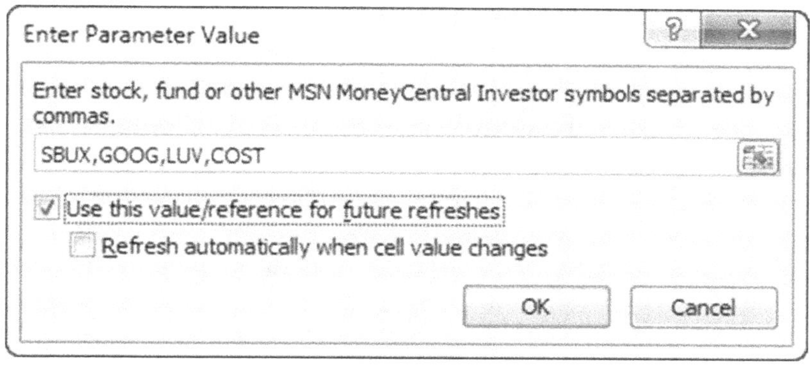

Click on "Use this value/reference for future refreshes". Then click OK.

Your tab will then look like this:

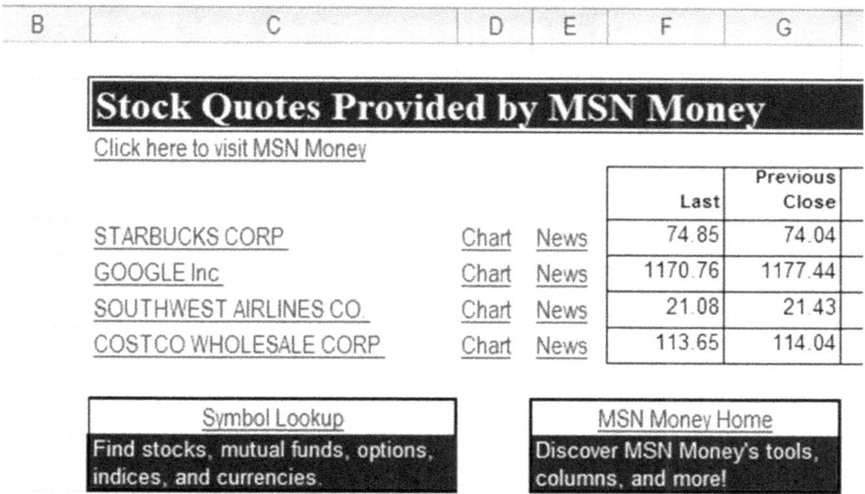

			Last	Previous Close
STARBUCKS CORP	Chart	News	74.85	74.04
GOOGLE Inc	Chart	News	1170.76	1177.44
SOUTHWEST AIRLINES CO.	Chart	News	21.08	21.43
COSTCO WHOLESALE CORP	Chart	News	113.65	114.04

There is even more data that is pulled in, but you get the idea. So if you own 100 shares of Starbucks, you can keep track of the value of that stock times the most current price as shown in this table. For example, in cell A6, you can type the number of shares you own for each of these stocks. Then starting in cell B6, you can create a formula that takes the stocks you own times the last price. Now the sheet looks like this:

B6 fx =+A6*F6

	A	B	C	D	E	F
1	Total Val	12786.68				
2						
3	Own	Value	Stock Quotes Provided by MSN Mon			
4			Click here to visit MSN Money			
5						Last
6	100	7482	STARBUCKS CORP	Chart	News	74.82
7	2	2341.72	GOOGLE Inc	Chart	News	1170.86
8	54	1142.64	SOUTHWEST AIRLINES CO.	Chart	News	21.16
9	16	1820.32	COSTCO WHOLESALE CORP	Chart	News	113.77

I added the "Total Val" and added up all of the values of the different stocks. Now, you can add stocks to your assets list, like this:

B	C	D	E	F	G	H	I
	Assets					Liabilities	
Name	My Bal	Bank Bal	Not Cleared		Name	Due	Balance
Checking	2100	2200	100				
Home	350000				Home	2000	200000
Car	6000				Car	200	2000
Stocks	12786.68				Credit Carc	25	1500
Total	370886.7				Total		203500
					Net Worth		167386.7

The stoks value is coming from the "Stocks" tab and because of how we set it up, the total assets changed automatically and the net worth changed automatically.

Here is the cool part, any time you want the stock prices to update, all you have to do is to click on the "Refersh All" icon as shown on the screenshot:

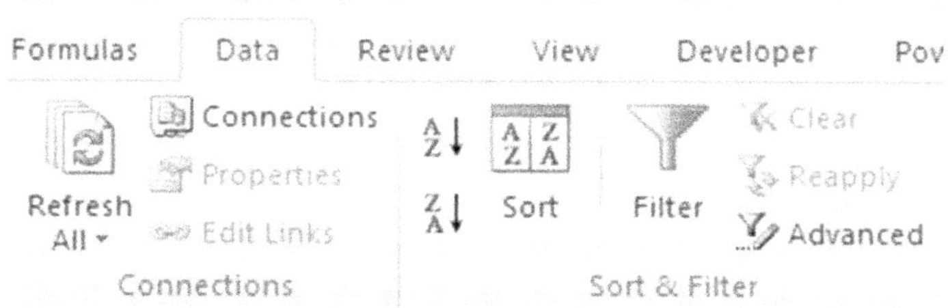

When you click on that, if you have one or ten connections set up, they will all refresh to the lastest stock prices and your net worth will change automatically as well.

Excel: Summary

There are so many things you can do with Excel, and these are the basics to get started. If you friend me on Facebook I can add you to the "Lifelong "L-Earning" Facebook Page and we can help each other to **L-EARN**!

ABOUT THE AUTHOR

Dr Julie Bonner lives in the Seattle, WA area. Dr Bonner was born in Mississippi and grew up in Alabama and thus has a rich southern heritage. From the storytelling tradition of the south, her teaching style is very practical and straightforward to help you move forward with small steps toward financial success in the long term. Dr Bonner teaches at University of Phoenix online and at the local University of Phoenix campus located in Tukwila, WA. Dr Bonner can be reached at jrbonner10@gmail.com for information on personal one on one coaching to build your tracking tools, or to build a tailored workshop for your group.

Facebook page dedicated to conversation about the book – connect with Dr Bonner through her email address and then request to be a part of the group on Lifelong L-Earning. You can learn from each other and come and go as you go through your financial planning journey.

www.ingramcontent.com/pod-product-compliance
Lightning Source LLC
Chambersburg PA
CBHW072313210326
41519CB00057B/4978

* 9 7 8 0 9 8 9 2 0 3 9 4 4 *